Seven Wonders of
ENGINEERING

Ron Miller

TWENTY-FIRST CENTURY BOOKS

Minneapolis

To Joel Turner Forrest Layne

Twenty-First Century Books
A division of Lerner Publishing Group, Inc.
241 First Avenue North
Minneapolis, MN 55401 U.S.A.

Website address: www.lernerbooks.com

Library of Congress Cataloging-in-Publication Data

Miller, Ron, 1947–
    Seven wonders of engineering / by Ron Miller.
        p.   cm. — (Seven wonders)
    Includes bibliographical references and index.
    ISBN 978–0–7613–4237–3 (lib. bdg. : alk. paper)
    1. Civil engineering—Juvenile literature. I. Title.
    TA149.M55 2010
    624—dc22   2009020322

Manufactured in the United States of America
1 – DP – 12/15/09

Contents

Introduction —— *4*

1 Empire State Building —— *7*

2 Panama Canal —— *17*

3 Golden Gate Bridge —— *27*

4 Channel Tunnel —— *37*

5 Saturn V Rocket —— *45*

6 Three Gorges Dam —— *55*

7 Nanomachines —— *63*

Timeline —— *70*
Choose an Eighth Wonder —— *72*
Glossary —— *73*
Source Notes —— *74*
Selected Bibliography —— *75*
Further Reading and Websites —— *76*
Index —— *78*

INTRODUCTION

*P*EOPLE LOVE TO MAKE LISTS OF THE BIGGEST AND THE BEST. ALMOST TWENTY-FIVE HUNDRED YEARS AGO, A GREEK WRITER NAMED HERODOTUS MADE A LIST OF THE MOST AWESOME THINGS EVER BUILT BY PEOPLE. THE LIST INCLUDED BUILDINGS, STATUES, AND OTHER OBJECTS THAT WERE LARGE, WONDROUS, AND IMPRESSIVE. LATER, OTHER WRITERS ADDED NEW ITEMS TO THE LIST. WRITERS EVENTUALLY AGREED ON A FINAL LIST. IT WAS CALLED THE SEVEN WONDERS OF THE ANCIENT WORLD.

The list became so famous that people began imitating it. They made other lists of wonders. They listed the Seven Wonders of the Modern World and the Seven Wonders of the Middle Ages. People even made lists of undersea wonders and the wonders of outer space.

Almost all the traditional ancient wonders were designed and built by ancient engineers. They employed the best tools, materials, and knowledge of their time to build the most impressive structures imaginable.

WHAT IS ENGINEERING?

Engineers take the discoveries of scientists and mathematicians to make practical things. People use these things every day. In ancient times, engineers built everything from roads and bridges to weapons.

In modern times, engineers still build roads, bridges, and big buildings. They also build cars, dams, airplanes, spacecraft, and tunnels. There are all kinds of engineers. Electronic engineers design and build everything from television sets to computers. Chemical engineers research new uses for plastics and other materials. Other engineers design new energy sources and nonpolluting factories.

Modern engineers use their knowledge of science and materials to build some of the most impressive structures ever seen on Earth—or off Earth. The pages that follow list seven wonders of modern engineering. They are some of the biggest and some of the smallest things humans have ever built. All of them are a combination of science and the need to make things people can use.

Welcome to the wonders of engineering.

This huge engine is one of five that propelled a Saturn V rocket in 1968.

1 Empire State BUILDING

$\mathcal{T}$ALL BUILDINGS ARE NOTHING NEW. FOR THOUSANDS OF YEARS, THE GREAT PYRAMID AT GIZA, EGYPT, WAS THE TALLEST STRUCTURE EVER BUILT BY HUMANS. IT IS 481 FEET (147 METERS) HIGH. LATER, PEOPLE BUILT TALLER CHURCHES. ONE WAS THE 495-FOOT-TALL (151 M) SAINT MARY'S CHURCH IN STRALSUND, GERMANY, BUILT IN 1625. THE WASHINGTON MONUMENT, AT 555 FEET (169 M), WAS THE TALLEST STRUCTURE IN THE WORLD WHEN IT WAS ERECTED IN WASHINGTON, D.C., IN 1884. THIS RECORD WAS BROKEN WHEN THE EIFFEL TOWER IN PARIS, AT 1,024 FEET (312 M), OPENED IN 1889. FOR THE NEXT FORTY-ONE YEARS, IT WAS THE TALLEST BUILDING ON EARTH.

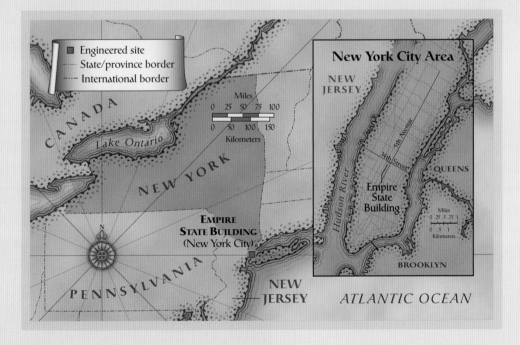

New York's Flatiron Building, originally called the Fuller Building, opened to businesses in 1902.

In the late 1920s, people competed to build the tallest building in the world. The race took place in New York City. This city was already famous for tall buildings, though none as tall as the Eiffel Tower. For instance, the Flatiron Building was one of the first skyscrapers in New York. Built in 1902, it is 285 feet (87 m) tall. Two businessmen, Walter Chrysler, of the Chrysler Corporation, and John Raskob, founder of General Motors, led the race.

THE INVENTION OF THE *Skyscraper*

Until the end of the nineteenth century, walls were made of brick or stone. The walls supported all the weight of the building. The taller a building was, the thicker the walls at its base had to be. If a building was tall, its first floors needed very thick walls. On really tall buildings, there might not be space for any rooms at all. The tallest brick building ever built was Philadelphia City Hall. Completed in 1901, it is 548 feet (167 m) tall.

Engineers developed a new way of constructing buildings in the 1880s. They were raised over a steel frame. A steel-framed building is supported by an internal steel framework. This is similar to the way a human body is supported by its skeleton. The building's walls, which support no weight, can be fairly thin. They can also be made of almost any material, including glass. A steel frame also allows buildings to be built to almost any height. The first skyscraper built with a steel frame was erected in 1885 in Chicago. It was 138 feet (42 m) tall. It is often thought of as the first true skyscraper.

MAKING SKYSCRAPERS *Possible*

Buildings as tall as the Empire State Building would not have been possible if they only had stairs. No one would live or work in a building where they had to climb up and down many flights of stairs every day. But Elisha Graves Otis had a new invention, the safety elevator *(below)*. He first showed it at the Crystal Palace Exposition in New York in 1854. This invention changed everything. Elevators made it possible to construct extremely tall buildings.

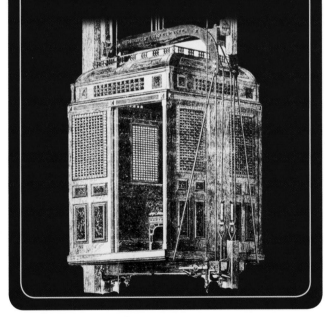

Chrysler announced his building first. Construction began in 1928. The following year, Raskob formed a special company called Empire State, Inc. The purpose of the company was to erect the tallest building in the world. One big problem was that Chrysler was keeping the final height of his building a secret. Raskob had no idea how tall his building needed to be to beat Chrysler. This did not keep him from starting, however.

DESIGNING SOMETHING NEW

Raskob turned to architect William Lamb to design his building. According to legend, Lamb asked Raskob how tall he wanted his new building to be. Raskob stood a pencil on end. He then asked, "Bill, how high can you make it so that it won't fall down?" No one knows if this story is true. But Lamb based his final design on the clean, straight lines of a pencil.

Chrysler's building had many months head start. So Raskob began a crash program to get his building going. The architects drew plans for the building in just two weeks. These were not the final plans, however. The designing process continued even during construction. Raskob still had no idea how tall his building needed to be. But Lamb had come up with a clever idea. Every floor of the building was to be

Above: *A truck climbs a ramp out of the excavated foundations of the Empire State Building in 1930.* **Inset:** *John Raskob* (left) *and New York governor Alfred Smith* (right) *examine a model of the Empire State Building.*

exactly the same. Extra floors could be easily added during construction. It would be like stacking a column of coins.

STARTING WORK

Excavation at the site on 350 Fifth Avenue began on January 22, 1930. Three hundred men worked day and night. They had to dig through hard granite bedrock to create the foundation. Construction started on March 17.

Meanwhile, Lamb had come up with a simple plan that he hoped would speed construction. He placed all the heat and air circulation ducts, mail chutes, plumbing and toilets, elevator shafts, and hallways in the center of the building. Offices would surround this space. To speed up the project, workers assembled windows, window frames, and girders at the site. The girders and beams were numbered with their location in the building. Workers only had to put them into place and rivet them together. Lamb even invented a way to handle more than ten million bricks. Trucks dumped the bricks into a large, tapered container. When workers needed bricks, they could release them from the bottom of the container into carts.

Once the foundation was ready, the steel skeleton of the building went up. Large cranes mounted on the upper floors lifted the heavy girders to the top. To move materials easily, workers built a special miniature railway at the construction site. They pushed their carts along the tracks. Each cart held eight times as much as an ordinary wheelbarrow. In this way, materials moved from one part of the work site to another more quickly. In another plan to save time, the unfinished building had its own restaurants. The thirty-five hundred workers would not have to come down from the upper floors to eat.

So many different people working at the same time meant every aspect had to be perfectly timed. With this timing, the framework of the building rose at the amazing rate of nearly four and a half floors a week. Workers even completed fourteen and a half floors in just ten working days. This record has never been beaten.

Workers finish the exterior of the Empire State Building's lower floors while cranes lift girders to frame the building's fortieth story.

NEARING THE FINISH LINE

This speed of construction was amazing. But the race wasn't to see who was going to finish his building first. The winner would be the man who built the tallest one. Raskob still did not know how tall the Chrysler Building was going to be.

Photographer Lewis W. Hine documented the dangerous conditions faced by construction workers on the Empire State Building. Hine photographed a steelworker tightening bolts (left) in 1930. The photo captures the Chrysler Building in the skyline behind him. His 1931 picture (below) of a riveter balanced on a narrow platform shows workers tending to many different stages of construction of the Empire State Building at once.

A tall spire topped the Chrysler Building, increasing its height dramatically as construction ended.

- **Total height: 1,453 feet (443 m) to the top of the lightning rod**
- **Floors: 102**
- **Weight: 365,000 tons (331,122 metric tons)**
- **Cost: $40.9 million (including land); $24.7 million (excluding land)**
- **Windows: 6,500**
- **Elevators: 73 (including 6 freight elevators) operating at speeds from 600 to 1,000 feet (180 to 300 meters) per minute**

"We thought we would be the tallest at eighty stories," said Hamilton Weber, the project manager. "Then the Chrysler went higher, so we lifted the Empire State to eighty-five stories, but only four feet [1.2 m] taller than the Chrysler. Raskob was worried that Walter Chrysler would pull a trick—like hiding a rod in the spire and then sticking it up at the last minute."And that's exactly what Chrysler did.

On May 28, 1930, a year before the Empire State Building was to be completed, Chrysler workers pushed the final section of a slender 27-ton (24-metric-ton) spire of stainless steel through the top of the building. The extra height of the spire made the Chrysler Building the tallest in the world. It was also the first human-made structure to stand taller than 1,000 feet (305 m). And it was 48 feet (15 m) taller than the announced height of the Empire State Building.

"In that giant shaft [the Empire State Building], I see a groping toward beauty and spiritual vision."
—Helen Keller, vision and hearing impaired writer and lecturer, after attending the opening ceremonies of the Empire State Building on May 1, 1931

> *"This achievement justifies pride of accomplishment in everyone who has had any part in its conception and construction and it must long remain one of the outstanding glories of a great city."*
>
> —*President Herbert Hoover, May 1, 1931*

Raskob immediately called for the redesign of his building. Raskob's architects told him they could make the Empire State Building at least eighty-five stories tall. This was eight stories taller than the Chrysler's seventy-seven. It had to be that much taller to beat the extra height of the Chrysler Building's spire. When it was completed in 1931, the Empire State Building had 102 stories. It was the first building in the world to have more than 100 stories. A solid gold rivet finished the task.

The Empire State Building was the tallest building in the world for forty-one years. The record was broken in 1986 by the 1,368-foot-tall (417 m) World Trade Center towers. (They were destroyed by terrorists on September 11, 2001.) Other buildings have since passed even that height. The Sears Tower (renamed

Visitors get an amazing view of the New York skyline from the deck on the tower's eighty-sixth floor.

ANOTHER RACE to the Sky

For more than thirty years, the New York Road Runners, a club of footrace fans, have held the annual Empire State Building Run Up *(below)*. Every year hundreds of people race up the 1,576 steps to the eighty-sixth floor observation deck. The record is held by a man who did it in less than ten minutes!

The lights that illuminate the Empire State Building are usually white, but they change on holidays. Here, red and green lights decorate the tower for Christmas.

the Willis Tower in 2009) in Chicago is 1,450 feet (442 m) tall. The Petronas Towers in Kuala Lumpur, Malaysia, is 1,483 feet (452 m) tall. The Taipei 101, in Taipei, Taiwan, is 1,667 feet (508 m), and newer buildings are exceeding that. But the Empire State Building set a standard for tall buildings. It also helped pioneer special construction techniques. These techniques made it possible to construct tall buildings inexpensively, quickly and, most important, safely.

The Empire State Building has become a symbol of New York City. It has starred in many movies, from *King Kong* to *Sleepless in Seattle*. It is one of the most visited buildings in the world. About 3.5 million people visit the building every year. Most take the elevator to the observation deck on the eighty-sixth floor to view the surrounding city.

2 Panama Canal

The Panama Canal is a series of natural lakes and rivers connected by artificial channels. It is one of the most important shipping routes in the world.

$\mathcal{G}$OLD WAS DISCOVERED IN CALIFORNIA IN 1848. PEOPLE WHO WANTED TO TRAVEL THERE FROM THE EAST COAST OF THE UNITED STATES HAD TWO CHOICES. THEY COULD TRAVEL CROSS-COUNTRY. OR THEY COULD GO BY SHIP. THE JOURNEY FROM NEW YORK TO SAN FRANCISCO IS ABOUT 3,000 MILES (4,828 KILOMETERS) BY LAND. IT IS 14,000 MILES (22,500 KM) BY WATER. THE CHOICE SEEMED EASY. BUT IN 1848, NO RAILROAD CROSSED THE CONTINENT. A COAST-TO-COAST TRAVELER WOULD HAVE TO GO BY HORSE OR WAGON TRAIN. THIS COULD TAKE MORE THAN SIX MONTHS.

This drawing shows the Flying Cloud *loading cargo for the sea voyage from New York City to San Francisco. Built in 1851, the* Flying Cloud *sailed until 1874.*

In the 1850s, one out of every fifteen travelers died of disease, accident, or attacks from Native Americans or bandits. By comparison, the journey by sea could take as little as ninety-eight days. It could be made in relative comfort and safety. A ship called the *Flying Cloud* made the journey in 1853 in just eighty-nine days. This record stood until 1989.

The sea journey was still a long one. Ships had to travel down the entire east coasts of the United States and South America. They rounded stormy Cape Horn and the southern tip of South America. Then they sailed back up the west coasts of South America and the United States. Many people saw that a shortcut would chop thousands of miles and months of travel from the journey. They knew just where this shortcut would be.

THE SHORTCUT

North America is attached to South America by the narrow strip of land called Central America. People thought this was the place to cut a canal. If it could be done, the journey from New York to California could be made much shorter. Engineers suggested many plans. One plan involved building a canal through the country of Nicaragua.

However, the narrowest part of Central America is the strip called the Isthmus of Panama. There the Atlantic Ocean and the Pacific Ocean are between 37 and 100 miles (60 and 161 km) apart. If a ship could travel across that narrow point, the ocean trip between New York and San Francisco could be cut in half. In 1869 a railroad finally linked the United States from coast to coast. Merchants still needed a passageway through Panama, however. Ships were the most practical way to transport cargo.

Many people proposed many schemes. One idea would transport the ship's passengers by railroad from one side of Panama to the other. Another scheme called for a special train that would carry entire ships, cargo and all, over the isthmus. But the only practical idea was to build a canal.

The French had built a successful canal, the Suez Canal, in Egypt in 1869. They next looked to Panama and started digging a canal there in 1880. The person in charge was Ferdinand de Lesseps. He was the engineer responsible for the Egyptian canal. But after more than 21,900 workers died—mostly from disease—the French abandoned the project.

Below: *A French crew in Panama works alongside an excavating machine in the early 1880s. Machines helped to move the water-soaked dirt, but they broke down frequently.* Inset: *Ferdinand de Lesseps served as a diplomat in Africa and Europe before coming to Panama to take charge of canal construction.*

TRYING AGAIN

At the beginning of the twentieth century, U.S. president Theodore Roosevelt wanted to make the United States a world power. To do this, the U.S. Navy had to have access to two oceans. Urged by Roosevelt, the United States bought the canal project from France. The price was $40 million. Roosevelt had engineer John Findley Wallace survey Panama to see if building a canal was practical. He decided that it was. Roosevelt put John Frank Stevens in charge of the project.

Stevens was determined not to repeat the mistakes the French had made. The French planned to create a sea-level canal. This would have provided an open passageway from one ocean to the other, similar to the Suez Canal. But there was one problem. The area of Panama where the canal was to be built has mountains nearly 1,000 feet (300 m) above sea level. Building a sea-level canal would mean digging down to sea level for about 40 miles (64 km). This would be an almost impossible task. Instead, Stevens chose to build a canal based on a system of locks and dams. The locks would allow ships to safely pass through the canal by gradually lifting or lowering them to the proper water level.

Stevens resigned in 1907, and Roosevelt appointed George Washington Goethals as his replacement. Goethals

John Frank Stevens began his career as a railroad worker. As a civil engineer, he helped build the Great Northern Railway from Minnesota to Washington in the 1890s.

CREATING A
New Nation

When the United States began to take an interest in building a canal, Panama was still part of the country of Colombia. The United States started negotiations for the rights to build a canal, but Colombia backed out. Theodore Roosevelt then supported Panama when it decided to become independent. Panama declared its independence from Colombia on November 3, 1903. The new nation immediately gave the Americans the rights to build the canal.

Locks and *Canals*

A lock is a kind of elevator for ships. It is an enclosure large enough to contain an entire vessel, with high sides and watertight gates at either end. To go from a higher water level to a lower one, a boat enters the lock through one of the gates. The gate closes behind it. Water drains out of the lock until it is at the same level as the next stretch of canal. The gate in front opens, and the boat continues on its way. To go to a higher level, the process is reversed. The boat enters the lock, and the gates close. Water is pumped in until the level is the same as the stretch of canal ahead.

Above: *A huge cruise ship waits in the Miraflores Locks on the Panama Canal. The locks have two channels each to handle more traffic.* Below: *Laborers work on the giant gates of the Gatun Locks in 1910. Each door of the steel gate stands 65 feet (20 m) tall and is 7 feet (2 m) thick.*

worked on the canal for the next seven years. He oversaw the digging of the enormous trench that was the canal itself. He also created several large artificial lakes to provide a source of water for the locks.

A BIG TASK AHEAD

Digging a canal through a strip of land that is only 50 miles (80 km) wide might not seem like such a big problem. But Panama offered unusual and dangerous difficulties. It is a hot and rainy country with rugged mountains, thick jungle, and deep swamps. Heavy rains could wash away weeks of hard work. Worse were deadly diseases, such as yellow fever and malaria. These were the very diseases that had put an end to the French attempt to dig a canal.

Stevens was aware of the problems with disease. He made certain that his workers had clean water and housing. A recent medical discovery had shown that mosquitoes spread yellow fever. Stevens's team took proper precautions, including covering windows with screening. They were able to eliminate yellow fever from Panama. In the ten years it took to build the U.S. canal, 5,609 workers died, compared to more than 20,000 French losses.

A worker spreads insecticide in a drainage ditch in Panama. By making it impossible for mosquitoes to breed in standing water near human workplaces and residences, Stevens's team reduced the spread of mosquito-borne diseases.

Left: *Dynamite crews prepare explosives during the excavation of the Culebra Cut.* Right: *Workers use shovels to finish excavations after steam shovels dug the main channel of the Culebra Cut.*

THE BIGGEST JOB

What sets the Panama Canal apart as a special wonder of modern engineering is the Culebra Cut. This is an 8.8-mile (14 km) channel cut through the rugged mountains that run down the spine of Panama.

Workers used thousands of tons of explosives to break up the hard rock and clay. Giant steam-powered shovels loaded the rock onto railcars to be hauled away. Many of the machines used in digging the Culebra Cut were invented or improved for this purpose. One was the machine that unloaded the dirt and rock from the railcars. The twenty giant unloaders, with 120 operators, did the work of 5,666 men unloading by hand. Another machine could hoist a whole section of railroad track—rails and ties—and swing it into position. Operated by twelve men, it did the work of six hundred.

More than 100 million cubic yards (76 cu. m) of rock and dirt were hauled away from the excavation site and dumped. Huge dams were constructed from some of this material. They held back the artificial lakes. One of the dams, Gatun Dam, was the largest earthen dam in the world. The lake that formed behind it was the largest artificial body of water in the world. Some of the debris from the cut was dumped into the sea at the Atlantic and Pacific ends. It created islands that protected the entrances to the canal. Material dumped in

Above: *Gatun Dam draws water from the artificial Gatun Lake to control the water level for the Panama Canal.* **Inset:** *In 1913 the tugboat Gatun was the first boat to use the Gatun Locks and enter the unfinished canal.*

the Pacific Ocean created the 500-acre (200-hectare) site for the city of Balboa.

In all, more than 268 million cubic yards (205 million cu. m) of material had to be dug out to create the Panama Canal. This would equal 53,600 football fields, each filled 3 feet (1 m) deep with dirt and rock.

The first ship passed through the completed canal on January 7, 1914. Since then more than 830,000 ships have used it. In recent times, more than 14,000 ships pass through it each year, carrying more than 203 million tons (184 metric tons) of cargo to all parts of the world.

"A finer body of men has never been gathered by any nation than the men who have done the work of building the Panama Canal."

—former president Theodore Roosevelt, 1913

PANAMA CANAL *Facts*

- The final cost of the canal was $336.7 million.
- About thirty-seven ships pass through the canal each day.
- The trip takes 8 to 10 hours.
- Each lock door weighs 750 tons (680 metric tons).
- About 52 million gallons (197 million liters) of water are used each time a lock is filled.
- The journey from New York to San Francisco was shortened by 7,872 miles (12,700 km).
- Adventurer and author Richard Halliburton swam through the canal in 1928. He paid a toll of 36 cents.

THE MODERN PANAMA CANAL

The original treaty with Panama gave the United States complete control over a 10-mile-wide (16 km) wide strip of land. It was called the Panama Canal Zone. The canal was built on U.S. soil and flew the U.S. flag. Citizens of Panama had to enter the zone as tourists. The zone had its own governor, police force, courts, shops, post offices, churches, and schools.

Panama protested this arrangement for many years. In 1977 U.S. president Jimmy Carter and Panama's general Omar Torrijos signed the Panama Canal Treaties. The treaties ended total U.S. control of the Panama Canal Zone. Instead, the canal would be operated by the Panama Canal Commission, an agency of the U.S. government. Finally, on December 31, 1999, the canal was turned over to Panama to operate.

Panamanian president Mireya Moscoso shakes hands with former U.S. president Jimmy Carter after signing the document putting the Panama Canal under Panama's control in 1999.

3 Golden Gate BRIDGE

The Golden Gate Bridge in San Francisco, California, glows orange on a sunny day. The engineers chose the color to make the bridge more visible on foggy days.

$\mathcal{T}$HE CITY OF SAN FRANCISCO, CALIFORNIA,

SITS AT THE END OF A LONG PENINSULA PUSHING INTO THE PACIFIC

OCEAN. IT IS SEPARATED FROM ALL THE CITIES TO THE EAST BY SAN

FRANCISCO BAY. TO THE NORTH LIES THE DEEP, RUSHING CURRENTS

OF A NARROW STRAIT CALLED THE GOLDEN GATE. IT SEPARATES SAN

FRANCISCO FROM THE CITIES TO THE NORTH.

For engineers, connecting the city to the east side of the bay was not especially difficult. They built a bridge across it. But bridging the Golden Gate was a special challenge. The channel is 1 to 2 miles (1.6 to 3 km) wide. It is more than 400 feet (120 m) deep. Pacific Ocean tides can rush through at speeds of up to 5.6 miles (9 km) per hour.

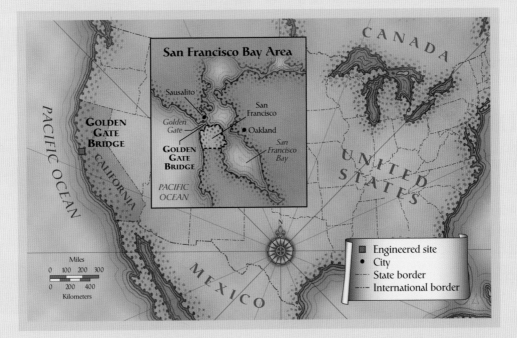

The currents this creates are powerful and dangerous. Crossing the strait by boat is extremely hazardous. Going completely around the bay is a journey of nearly 200 miles (320 km). Only 12 miles (20 km) separates San Francisco from the city of Sausalito on the other side of the Golden Gate.

A bridge across the strait was needed. But it would have to be an extraordinary bridge. First, it would have to span 1.3 miles (2 km) of the strait. It would have to stand up to powerful tides and currents, extremely deep water, and almost constant high winds. A bridge across the strait couldn't be allowed to interfere with the heavy ship traffic that passed through the Golden Gate. The bridge spanning it would have to be a suspension bridge. In the beginning of the twentieth century, no one knew how to build a suspension bridge that long.

THE DREAMER

No one took the idea of a bridge across the Golden Gate seriously. But in the early 1920s, an engineer named Joseph Strauss thought it might work. Strauss had to fight for his bridge for several years. Most people thought a bridge across the strait was either impossible or too expensive. California finally approved the project in 1924. The state bought the land on either side of the strait.

SUSPENSION *Bridges*

Unlike most other types of bridges, where the roadway is supported by columns or arches underneath, the roadway of a suspension bridge hangs from strong cables. The cables extend from one end of the bridge to the other and rest on top of high towers. They are secured at each end by heavy anchors. The anchors bear most of the weight of the bridge. Suspension bridges are the most difficult and expensive type of bridge to build, but they make it possible for engineers to span larger distances than with any other bridge design.

Joseph Strauss, shown here in 1930, designed drawbridges and lift bridges before submitting his plans for the Golden Gate Bridge.

Strauss, chief engineer of the bridge, hired many experts with experience in building big suspension bridges. Architect Irving Morrow designed the two towers that would support the bridge. Morrow also selected the distinctive color of the bridge—international orange—to complement the surrounding landscape. It also made it more visible in the fogs that so often cover the bay.

WORK BEGINS

Construction began on January 5, 1933. It took four and a half years to complete. In spite of the size and difficulty of the project, few lives were lost. This was largely because of Strauss's invention. He placed steel safety nets under the bridge to catch workers who might slip and fall. The nets caught and saved nineteen men.

One of the most important parts of the bridge is the massive anchors on either shore. These hold the ends of the cables that support the span. The entire weight of the bridge is held by the anchors. Strauss used more than 1 million tons (0.9 metric tons) of concrete to build them.

Above left: *Bridge workers stand in one of Strauss's safety nets high above the bay.*
Below left: *Workers direct a concrete pour on the bridge's north anchor point.*

Construction workers prepare to pour the concrete foundations of the bridge's southern pier around 1934. Muddy puddles are all that remain of the millions of gallons of seawater pumped out to make the work possible.

The two towers were built on piers that rest on the bottom of the Golden Gate strait. The northern pier sits solidly only 20 feet (6 m) below the water's surface. The southern pier, however, had to be built in the open Pacific Ocean. There the water is more than a 100 feet (30 m) deep. To build this pier, Strauss had to construct an enormous cofferdam to hold back the ocean water. This watertight box with high walls was big enough to contain a football field. The cofferdam kept the site dry. Workers then pumped in hundreds of tons of concrete to create the pier. The southern pier is bigger than the largest of the Egyptian pyramids. It required more concrete than the Empire State Building.

Once the piers and their towers were complete, the next step was to make the cables that held the roadway. The cables had to be strong enough to support the bridge. They also had to be flexible enough to allow the bridge to sway in the strong winds that blow through the strait. Each of the two main cables is more than 1 mile (1.6 km) long. They had to be custom-made on location. Huge looms wove heavy wire like the strands in a rope. The looms spun out the cable as it was stretched from shore to shore. It took more than six months to weave the two main cables.

Above: *Before the bridge's giant cables could be spun, workers had to build catwalks between the bridge towers. Below left: A cable loom makes its slow climb up the catwalk, leaving heavy cable behind it. Below right: Thousands of individual wires can be seen in this crosssection of the main bridge cable.*

GOLDEN GATE BRIDGE
MAIN SPAN
4200 FEET

LENGTH OF ONE CABLE .... 7650 FT. (2331.7m)
DIAMETER OF ONE CABLE ... 36⅜ IN. (92.4 cm)
WIRES IN EACH CABLE 27,572
TOTAL WIRE USED .... 80,000 MILES (128,748 km)
WEIGHT OF CABLE (SUSPENDED ACCESSORIES) .. 24,500 TONS (22,226 m.tons)

Cable Contractor: John A. Roebling's Sons Co.
Trenton & Roebling, New Jersey

Once the suspension cables were in place, workers built the steel base of the roadbed that would hang from it.

From the main cables, smaller support cables—called ropes—drop to the roadway. The bridge has 250 pairs of ropes, each 2.7 inches (6.8 centimeters) in diameter. They transfer the weight of the roadbed to the main cables. The main cables transfer the weight to the anchor blocks on the shores.

SUCCESS AT LAST

Work on the giant bridge went smoothly. It was completed in April 1937. Strauss finished the bridge five months late but $1.3 million under budget. His reward was a $1 million bonus and a lifetime pass to the bridge.

The bridge officially opened the following month. About two hundred thousand people made the first crossing on foot. The dedication ceremony was held the next day. An

GOLDEN GATE *Bridge Facts*

- The total length (including approaches) is 1.7 miles (8,981 feet, or 2,737 m).
- The length of the middle span is 4,200 feet (2,000 m).
- Each main cable is 7,650 feet (2,332 m) long and contains a total of 80,000 miles (129,000 km) of steel wire.
- The cables are 36.4 inches (0.9 m) in diameter.
- Its total weight is 887,000 tons (804,700 metric tons).
- Its average height above water is 220 feet (67 m).
- About 40 million cars a year cross the bridge.

"Standing at the gateway of the Pacific, at the crossroads of the redwood empire, a new Statue of Liberty . . . its face upturned to the sun, rich in promise and vibrant with eternal youth, the swift wings of the wind that caresses it shall beat to the farthest corners of the Earth its inspiring message to posterity forever."
—*Joseph Strauss, bridge dedication speech, 1937.*

Military planes fly between the towers of the Golden Gate Bridge during opening ceremonies in 1937.

official parade of automobiles featuring the mayor of San Francisco and other celebrities came afterward. The next day, President Franklin D. Roosevelt pushed a button in Washington, D.C., that signaled the official opening of the bridge.

For the next twenty-seven years, the Golden Gate Bridge was the longest suspension bridge in the world. In 1964 the Verrazano-Narrows Bridge in New York took the record. Its center span is 4,260 feet (1,298 m) long. Many larger suspension bridges have been built since. The center span of the Akashi Kaikyo Bridge in Japan, which opened in 1998, is 6,532 feet (1,991 m) long. This is one and half times as long as the Golden Gate Bridge.

Celebration!

The Golden Gate Bridge has been closed only three times because of the weather. It was closed a fourth time as part of the celebration of its fiftieth anniversary in 1987. On that day, the bridge was open only to pedestrians. Three hundred thousand people crowded onto the bridge to celebrate *(below)*.

Superbridges

Engineers continue to plan and build larger and longer bridges. The Bering Strait, which separates Alaska from Russia, has long tempted bridge builders. The 55-mile-long (89 km) bridge required to cross the strait would be twice as long as any bridge ever built. Engineers would also have to deal with severe weather and icebergs. Such a bridge, however, would allow a person to drive a car almost around the world. The car could go from the southern tip of South America through North America and across the Bering Strait to Asia and then all the way to Paris, France. And if another superbridge were to be built, the driver could continue on to London, England. This second superbridge would be across the 22-mile-wide (35 km) English Channel. One thing that might make future superbridges possible is the development of new materials that are stronger than steel.

But it's not size alone that makes the Golden Gate Bridge one of the architectural wonders of the world. It was also its innovative design. The design introduced new techniques that helped make future giant bridges possible. The bridge is a structure of such great beauty that it can be considered a work of art as much as a product of engineering genius.

4 Channel Tunnel

The Channel Tunnel exit opens in front of a train traveling from Great Britain to France.

$\mathcal{G}$REAT BRITAIN IS SEPARATED FROM CONTINENTAL EUROPE BY A STRETCH OF WATER 350 MILES (562 KM) LONG. BUT IT IS ONLY 21 MILES (34 KM) WIDE AT ITS NARROWEST POINT. MORE THAN NINE HUNDRED PEOPLE HAVE SWUM ACROSS THE ENGLISH CHANNEL. FOR CENTURIES THE ONLY OTHER WAY TO MAKE THE CROSSING WAS BY BOAT. THE CHANNEL WAS INCONVENIENT FOR TRAVELERS, BUT IT WAS A STRONG BARRIER TO BRITAIN'S ENEMIES.

In 1802, in a period of peace during a long war between Great Britain and France, someone suggested that a tunnel could connect France and England. It would not be very different from the shafts in ordinary coal mines. Horse- or donkey-driven carts could carry passengers through a narrow, candle-lit tunnel.

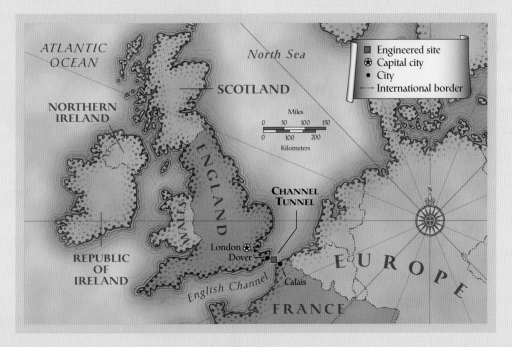

Before anyone could decide whether a tunnel might be possible, the war began again. The last thing anyone wanted was an easy way for an army to cross the channel.

NINETEENTH-CENTURY DREAMERS

By the end of the nineteenth century, engineers believed that nothing was beyond their powers. They had laid telegraph cables under the Atlantic Ocean. They had built vast railroads. Engineers had cut a great canal through Suez in Egypt. They had also dug long railroad tunnels. The longest was the 8.5 miles (14 km) long railway tunnel through Mount Cenis in the Swiss Alps. Digging this tunnel introduced such marvels as mechanical tunnel-boring machines, air-powered drills, and dynamite.

People again began thinking about a tunnel under the English Channel. In 1857 French engineer Thome De Gamond had suggested a plan for a rail tunnel to be bored through the bed of solid chalk he believed formed the bottom of the channel. Steam trains would run on a double track in a gas-lit tunnel. At the halfway point, the tunnel would come to the surface at an artificial island. But nothing came of these ideas.

The first serious attempt at creating a channel tunnel began in 1880. Workers used air-driven tunnel-boring machines

OVER THE *Channel*

On January 7, 1785, French balloonist Jean Pierre Blanchard and U.S. balloonist John Jeffries became the first people to cross the channel by air. They flew their hydrogen balloon *(below)* from Dover, England, to a spot not far from Calais, France. About 124 years later, a French pilot named Louis Blériot made the first crossing by airplane.

Right: *Thome De Gamond proposed this plan for a tunnel carrying steam trains between France and Britain.*
Below: *A visitor explores a tunnel abandoned after the British government cancelled tunneling attempts in 1882.*

like those that tunneled through the Alps. The project went very well. Tunnelers dug about 1.3 miles (2 km) of tunnel from both the French and British sides in just a few weeks. Planners hoped that within five years, electric-powered trains would be shuttling passengers back and forth through the 7-foot-diameter (2.1 m) tunnel. Unfortunately, many politicians in Britain worried about invasion and doomed the project again.

DREAMING ANEW

The two countries did not again seriously discuss the idea of a channel tunnel until nearly a century later. During World War II (1939–1945), German bombers easily crossed the channel by air. The English Channel was no longer a barrier to enemies. Tunneling began again in 1974. But leaders canceled the project a year later because of political opposition and lack of funds.

A new tunnel project began in 1987. This time, eight years later, in 1994, the first Channel Tunnel connecting France and England opened to the public. The project cost $12 billion. The tunnel is 32 miles (51 km) long. This

"I believe the commercial advantages of this Tunnel would be enormous."
—*William Gladstone, leader of the Liberal Party of Great Britain, 1888*

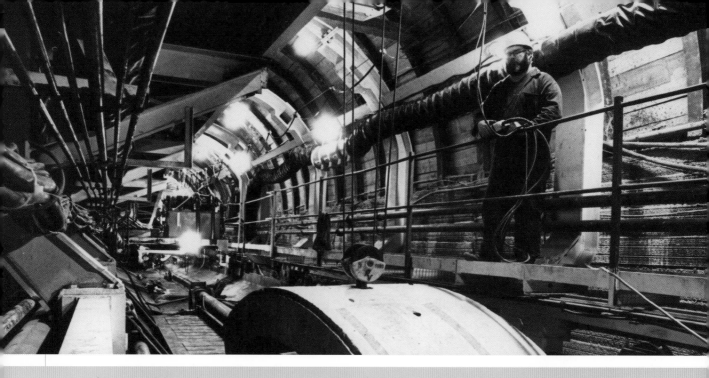

A construction worker prepares to raise a section of concrete wall during the 1974 attempt to build a tunnel beneath the English Channel. When the final tunneling effort began in 1987, workers on the British side used this tunnel as a starting point.

makes it the second-longest railway tunnel in the world. The only one longer is the 33-mile (53 km) Seikan Tunnel in Japan.

THREE TUNNELS

The Channel Tunnel is actually three separate tunnels. The two main railway tunnels, about 98 feet (30 m) apart, are separated by a smaller service tunnel. The service tunnel allows maintenance workers access to the main tunnels. It was the first to be constructed.

To build the tunnel, thirteen thousand laborers worked alongside eleven huge mechanical tunneling machines. A British team and a French team started from opposite sides of the channel at the same time. The largest tunnel-boring machines used in digging the Channel Tunnel weighed 1,200 tons (1,090 metric tons). It was 29 feet (8.8 m) in diameter. The cylinder-shaped machines were as long as two football fields. Huge, rotating, disk-shaped cutter heads ate into the rock. The machines cut through the rock at the rate of 15 feet (4.6 m) an hour. Conveyor belts carried the tons of crushed rock to the rear of the machine. By the time the tunnel was finished, 282 million cubic feet (8 million

Samphire Hoe

The British tunnelers excavated almost 5.2 million cubic yards (4 million cu. m) of chalk. This material was deposited near Shakespeare Cliff on the coast, creating a 90-acre (36-hectare) landscaped area known as Samphire Hoe *(below)*. It has become a popular place for walks, picnics, and fishing.

cu. m) of material had been removed. This would make a cube 656 feet (200 m) on each side.

The machines were followed by work crews who installed the concrete lining of the tunnel. The lining was formed of premade half cylinders that were fastened to the inside walls. It took 674,755 of these lining pieces to cover the tunnel walls.

With two teams boring tunnels from opposite directions, it was vital that they met exactly. If they didn't, the entire project would be ruined. Billions of dollars and years of work would be wasted. Finally, on December 1, 1990, a construction worker from the British side and one from the French side broke through and met. They shook hands.

Two of the Channel Tunnel's three tubes transport passengers and cargo. Engineers designed new cars especially for these tunnels. The smaller, central tube gives workers access to the travel tunnels to maintain the tunnels or to reach trains in need of repair.

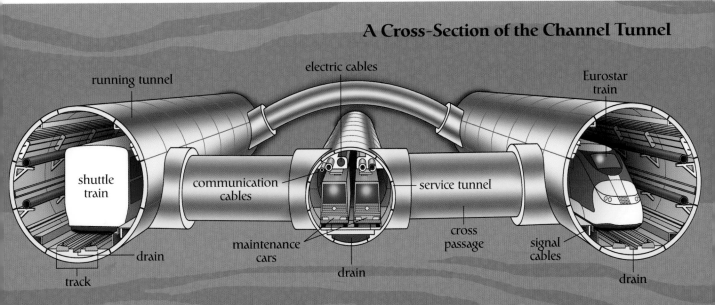

A Cross-Section of the Channel Tunnel

running tunnel

electric cables

Eurostar train

shuttle train

communication cables

service tunnel

maintenance cars

cross passage

signal cables

drain

track

drain

drain

Above: *One of the giant tunnel-boring machines moves into position during excavations.* Below left: In 1990, *French and British engineers make the first breakthrough connecting the tunnel's two ends.*

CHUNNEL *Facts*

- Building the tunnel required the labor of 13,000 engineers, technicians, and construction workers.
- The tunnels are 32 miles (51 km) long. Of that distance, 23 miles (38 km) are undersea.
- The undersea tunnels are an average of 164 feet (50 m) below the floor of the channel.
- Six tunnel-boring machines were used by the British and five by the French.
- Each machine was 656 feet (200 m) long.

A Eurostar train emerges from the Channel Tunnel on the French side. Since the tunnel opened, engineers have continued working on ways to make it a safer and more efficient route.

A Tunnel at Last

What was officially known as Eurotunnel—but more affectionately dubbed the Chunnel—opened in May 1994. Two types of electric trains operate in the tunnel. One type transports passengers and freight. It can travel at nearly 100 miles (160 km) per hour while hauling 2,100 tons (1,905 metric tons) of cargo. The other carries passengers and vehicles, including buses and trucks. It can reach speeds of 185 miles (298 km) per hour. Since the tunnel opened, trains have carried 3.5 million cars and buses, 1 million trucks, 8 million passengers, and 4 million tons (3.6 million metric tons) of freight.

What's next? Engineers are thinking about building that giant bridge over the channel.

"Today, for the first time, men can cross the Channel underground. What a brilliant sign of the vitality of our two countries."

—President François Mitterrand of France, 1990

5 *Saturn V* ROCKET

A Saturn V rocket awaits launch at the Kennedy Space Center in Cape Canaveral, Florida, in 1967.

$\mathcal{I}$N 1961 PRESIDENT JOHN F. KENNEDY SAID:

"I BELIEVE THAT THIS NATION SHOULD COMMIT ITSELF TO ACHIEVING

THE GOAL, BEFORE THIS DECADE IS OUT, OF LANDING A MAN ON

THE MOON AND RETURNING HIM SAFELY TO THE EARTH." LATER, HE

EXPLAINED TO THE PEOPLE OF THE UNITED STATES: "WE CHOOSE TO

GO TO THE MOON IN THIS DECADE AND DO THE OTHER THINGS, NOT

BECAUSE THEY ARE EASY, BUT BECAUSE THEY ARE HARD."

And hard it was. At the time, no rocket was big enough or powerful
enough to carry a crew of astronauts to the Moon. It would have to be
designed and built from scratch. No one had ever before attempted to
build a rocket so large.

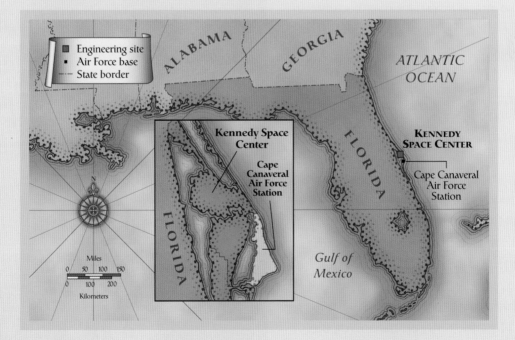

A MONSTER ROCKET

Engineers at the National Aeronautics and Space Administration's (NASA's) Marshall Space Flight Center in Alabama designed the Saturn V Moon rocket. It was a monster. Including the spacecraft attached to it, the Saturn V would tower more than 363 feet (111 m), taller than the Statue of Liberty. Fully loaded, the vehicle would weigh about 6.7 million pounds (3 million kg). By comparison, the rocket that launched the first American into space in 1961 was only 69 feet (21 m) tall and weighed just 61,207 pounds (27,763 kg). With more than three million parts, the Saturn V was too big to be built by one company. Four of the largest aerospace manufacturers in the United States worked together to build it.

One of the biggest challenges to the engineers was developing an engine that could lift a 6-million-pound (2.7 million kg) vehicle off the ground. They needed five of them, actually. The *V* in Saturn V stood for its five engines. When all five engines fired, they created 37 million horsepower. It's enough energy to light up New York City for seventy-five minutes. Every second the engines ran, they used 15 tons (14 metric tons) of fuel and oxidizer.

AN ANCIENT *Invention*

The Chinese invented rockets fired by gunpowder *(below)* more than one thousand years ago. One of the first recorded uses of rockets was in the battle at Kai-fung-fu in 1232. Soon afterward, the rocket made its way to the West, where Europeans quickly adapted them for military use. The word *rocket* comes from the Italian word *rochetta,* "a small spindle, a device to spin yarn." A rocket seems to resemble a spindle. Gunpowder-powered rockets were used to set off fireworks and for warfare. But the West did not take them very seriously. They were unreliable and not very powerful. Then, in 1926, U.S. physicist Robert H. Goddard invented a rocket powered by liquid fuel. With liquid fuel, more powerful rockets could reach tremendous speeds. These were the direct ancestors of the Saturn V.

German scientist Wernher von Braun, a pioneer of the United States space program, stands by the F-1 engines of the Saturn V rocket. Von Braun had been in charge of the development of the V-2 rocket for Germany during World War II. It was the largest, most powerful rocket ever built at the time. After the war, von Braun came to the United States. His knowledge of the V-2 became the basis for later rockets. One of these was the Jupiter C. It launched the United States's first satellite into space.

(Space rockets can't get enough oxygen from the thin air of space to burn their fuel. They carry their own oxidizer in special tanks.) The engines built for the Saturn V were called the F-1s. Not one ever failed.

The Saturn V was really three rockets, one stacked on top of another. The huge lower rocket, the first stage, used the mighty F-1 engines. Above that was a second stage with two smaller rocket engines. On top of that was the third stage with a single rocket engine, and on top of that was the *Apollo* spacecraft. The third stage of Saturn V carried the spacecraft into orbit around Earth and then sent it toward the Moon. Each stage detached as it used up its fuel and fell away.

"*It is a monster, that rocket . . . it has a life of its own.*"
—*Guenter Wendt, NASA engineer, 1968*

Top: *Scaffolding surrounds the first stage of a Saturn V rocket during assembly.* Middle: *A crane lowers the second stage of a Saturn V rocket onto the top of the first stage.* Bottom: *The third stage of a Saturn V rocket drops into place.*

Stages

The Saturn V rocket was built to have three stages to save weight and fuel. When a stage used up its fuel, it was dropped off. This meant less weight for the remaining rocket to carry. It also meant less fuel was needed overall. The entire rocket could be lighter and cheaper.

The first stage, powered by the five F-1 engines, took the rocket to an altitude (height above Earth) of 42 miles (68 km) in just two and a half minutes. It reached a speed of nearly 7,000 miles (11,000 km) per hour. Then the second stage ignited (began burning). It built on the earlier speed to reach 15,000 miles (24,140 km) per hour. This took the rocket to an altitude of 117 miles (188 km). The third and final stage then took over, putting the *Apollo* spacecraft into Earth orbit at an altitude of about 115 miles (185 km). It sent the spacecraft on course to the Moon before it dropped off.

A crawler (right) carries a Saturn V rocket from the Vehicle Assembly Building (left) to the launch site during a 1966 test of the launch facilities.

MORE THAN A ROCKET

To assemble the giant rocket, NASA had to erect the largest building in the world (in volume). The Vehicle Assembly Building is still the tallest building in the United States not in a city. Inside, it is a vast empty space. The 400-foot-tall (120 m) rocket could stand upright in it. To move the assembled Saturn V to its launch site, NASA engineers built two of the largest land vehicles on Earth. Known as crawlers, they are two stories high and ride on two pairs of enormous caterpillar treads. Two 2,750-horsepower diesel engines power them. The platform on top, which holds the rocket, is as big as a baseball diamond. Each crawler weighs 5.5 million pounds (2.5 million kg). They are so heavy they crush to dust the gravel surfaces on which they travel.

The crawler moves at only 1 mile (1.6 km) per hour. It didn't dare move any faster. Even a tiny wobble could have toppled the towering rocket. It took three hours to carry a Saturn V rocket to the launchpad. Forty years after the Apollo Moon program, the crawlers carry space shuttles to their launch sites.

BAR CODES

The bar codes familiar to every shopper were invented by NASA to keep track of the more than three million parts needed to construct the giant Saturn V rocket.

This series of photos shows the Saturn V rocket launching Apollo 11 *in 1969.*

The Saturn V was launched for the first time on November 9, 1967. It was as though a volcano had erupted in the middle of the Florida coast. The sound generated by the five huge F-1 engines was detected over 1,000 miles (1,600 km) away. During the launch, the roof of a nearby CBS television building collapsed.

NASA had ordered fifteen Saturn V rockets. NASA launched thirteen of them. Twelve were used in the Apollo Moon program between 1967 and 1972. One sent the Skylab space station into space in 1973. This was the last time a Saturn V rocket was used.

To the Moon

The first mission to the Moon took off from Earth on July 16, 1969. The spacecraft carried Neil Armstrong, Michael Collins, and Edwin "Buzz" Aldrin. On July 20, while Collins remained in the command module *Columbia* in orbit around the Moon, Armstrong and Aldrin, in the lunar lander *Eagle*, became the first humans to land on the Moon.

Left: *A trail of burning rocket fuel follows the first stage of the Saturn V rocket as it propels* Apollo 11 *into space.* Below: *Neil Armstrong* (left) *and Buzz Aldrin* (right) *plant a U.S. flag on the surface of the Moon.*

"That's one small step for [a] man; one giant leap for mankind."

Neil Armstrong, commander of the Apollo 11 Moon landing, July 20, 1969

A crawler leaves the Vehicle Assembly Building carrying the Apollo 15 spacecraft and its Saturn V rocket for a 1971 mission to the Moon. It carried the first lunar rover exploration vehicle.

The third stage of a Saturn V rocket stands on display at the Kennedy Space Center in Florida.

SATURN V *Facts*

- **A car that gets 30 miles to the gallon (12 km/liter) could travel around the world about two hundred times on the propellants used during the first Apollo lunar landing mission.**
- **The fully loaded Saturn V Moon rocket was 60 feet (18 m) taller than the Statue of Liberty and weighed thirteen times as much.**
- **The fuel pumps for the Saturn V's F-1 engines were as powerful as thirty diesel locomotives.**

INTO THE FUTURE

The remaining two Saturn V rockets are on display. One is at the U.S. Space and Rocket Center in Huntsville, Alabama, the rocket's birthplace. The other is on exhibit at the Kennedy Space Center in Florida.

President George W. Bush announced plans for future human missions to Mars in 2004. Some people suggested rebuilding the old Saturn V rocket for them. But technology has advanced a great deal in forty years. New materials and new manufacturing techniques have made the Saturn V outdated. Rockets just as powerful can be built smaller and more cheaply. The Ares V rocket is one example. NASA plans to use the Ares V to launch future Mars missions. The Ares V is even taller than the Saturn V. It will be capable of sending more than 286,000 pounds (130,000 kg) into orbit. This is far more than the Saturn V could carry. The Ares V will also have reusable boosters. The booster rockets of the Saturn V dropped off into space. The entire Saturn V was literally thrown away, stage by stage, once it was used.

6 Three Gorges DAM

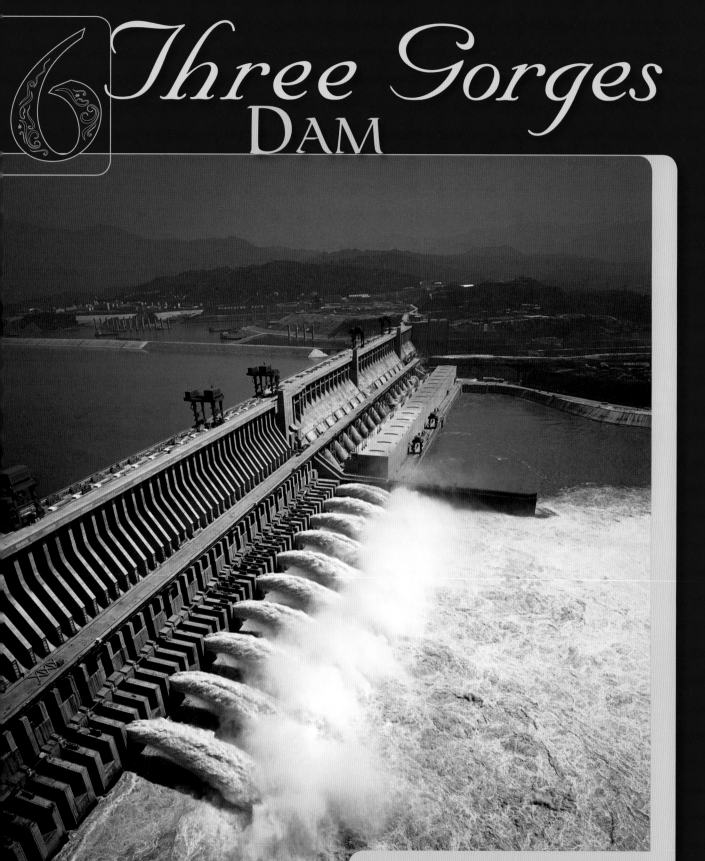

The waters of the Yangtze River flow through China's Three Gorges Dam. The enormous dam generates much of China's power and makes it possible for cargo ships to sail deep into the country's interior.

$\mathcal{N}$OT EVERY ENGINEERING WONDER IS POPULAR OR WELCOME. CHINA'S ENORMOUS THREE GORGES DAM ON THE YANGTZE RIVER IS ONE EXAMPLE. FROM ITS VERY BEGINNING, IT INVITED DEBATE FROM ALL ACROSS THE WORLD.

The project is the largest hydroelectric power station in the world. Hydroelectric power is generated by water pushing on turbines. These are machines that generate electricity. The Three Gorges Dam generates one-ninth of all the power used in China. The dam itself is 6,500 feet (2,000 m) wide and 606 feet (185 m) tall. The lake behind it is hundreds of feet deep and more than 350 miles (560 km) long. By using a system of locks—the largest ever built—oceangoing freighters are able to sail 1,500 miles (2,400 km) into the interior of China. A city upriver from the dam has a population of more than 30 million people.

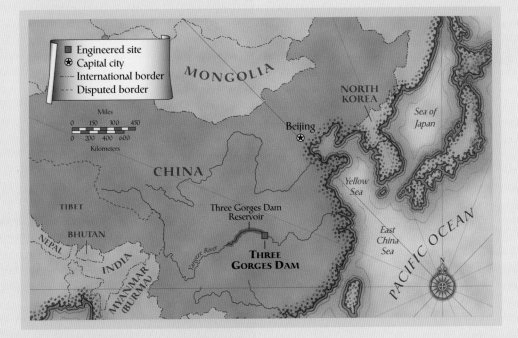

A boat sails through the Three Gorges on the Yangtze River. The area is known for its beautiful scenery and abundant wildlife.

With the increase in shipping through the dam, this city has become the major manufacturing center of China. The dam also helps control flooding by controlling the flow of the river. The Yangtze has produced devastating floods for thousands of years. In the past century alone, these floods have claimed more than one million lives. But damming the third-longest river in the world was not an easy job.

THE WONDERS of China

The Three Gorges Dam is not the only great engineering wonder in China. It is only the newest. The Great Wall, which stretches for more than 4,000 miles (6,437 km), was built between the fifth century B.C. and the sixteenth century A.D. It was intended to protect the northern borders of China from invasion. The Grand Canal of China is the longest ancient canal in the world. Parts of it date to the fifth century B.C. It stretches nearly 1,114 miles (1,790 km) between the cities of Beijing and Hangzhou. In Beijing is the Forbidden City, the ancient emperor's palace of China. It is the largest ancient palace in the world. It was built over a period of five hundred years and has more than ten thousand rooms.

China also has many modern architectural wonders. One is the "bird's nest" stadium built for the 2008 Summer Olympics. Another is the Beijing National Grand Theater, one of the largest indoor theaters in the world. The theater resembles an enormous egg sitting in the middle of a lake.

Engineers first suggested damming the Yangtze in 1919. During the 1950s, the Chinese government ordered studies to see if the project was possible. In 1970 engineers erected a small dam as a test for the future full-scale Three Gorges Dam. This small dam started generating power in 1981. The Chinese government gave the go-ahead for the Three Gorges project in December 1994.

Forty thousand workers labored on the huge project. First, they moved 134 million cubic yards (102 million cu. m) of stone and earth from the gorges. Then they began building the dam itself. They used 11 million tons (10 million metric tons) of cement, 1.9 million tons (1.7 million metric tons) of rolled steel, and 1.6 million tons (1.5 million metric tons) of timber. The finished dam stands 606 feet (185 m) high. It is 6,500 feet (2,000 m), or more than 1.2 miles (2 km) wide.

During construction of the Three Gorges Dam, workers leveled the bottom of the riverbed and built the massive steel and concrete structures that would later hold power-generating equipment.

Above left: *Workers watch as cranes deliver concrete during construction of the Three Gorges Dam in 2001. Below left: Water gushes out of the dam's power plant. Below right: Cargo ships line up in a lock at the Three Gorges Dam in 2006.*

A lake holding nearly 1.5 million cubic feet (42,500 cu. m) of water stands behind the dam. The water passes through twenty-six turbines to generate 18 gigawatts of electricity. This is nine times as much as the Hoover Dam in the United States. It is enough power to supply more than three cities the size of New York for an entire year.

Workers recover scrap metal from houses along the Yangtze River. The owners of the houses were forced to move away in anticipation of rising water levels caused by the dam.

CONTROVERSY

The arguments about the dam concern its impact on the environment and people. As many as 13 cities, 140 towns, 1,352 villages, 657 factories, and 74,131 acres (30,000 hectares) of farmland disappeared under the waters of the reservoir. More than 1.3 million people lost their homes and had to move.

The waters of the dam also flooded many mines and waste dumps. Metals and trash from the mines and dumps polluted the lake. The river carried waste and sewage from large industrial cities upstream into the lake. The Three Gorges lake is one of the most polluted bodies of water on the planet.

Water soaking into unstable land on either side of the dam has caused landslides and erosion. This has added more pollution and sediment to the river. This

Three Gorges Dam

Garbage washes up on the shore of the Yangtze River near the Three Gorges Dam.

An End to *Dams?*

Dams were once symbols of progress. But in recent years, dams have also become symbols of environmental and social problems. This is because many big dams were built with little thought for the impact they would have on the land and people around them. Dams control floods, provide water for irrigation, and generate power. But they also affect fish migration and animal habitats. The lake behind a dam floods huge areas of land. In addition to the loss of land, these lakes can also cause increased erosion. That's why fewer big dams are being built and some older dams are being removed.

polluted water eventually makes its way to the East China Sea. The pollution is killing fish that live in the sea. One million tons (0.9 metric tons) of fish a year may be lost.

The flooding of the Three Gorges section of the Yangtze River has drowned some of the most famous scenery in China. It has also covered many important historical sites. Before the flooding, sixty-four teams of archaeologists worked to save ancient tombs, temples, and villages. They were able to dismantle and move some sites, such as the Zhangfei Temple and Dachang Ancient Town. But the teams could only study others before the waters closed over them forever.

Is the Three Gorges Dam a success? Yes and no. The dam has enabled China to increase its electrical output by 10 percent. This means China doesn't

Above: *Floodwaters rise over centuries-old inscriptions carved into the cliffs at Qutang Gorge.* Inset: *An archaeologist cleans pots found in an ancient gorge gravesite. Researchers raced to document the site before it flooded.*

have to build new coal-fired power plants that cause air pollution. But does the decrease of pollution created by coal balance the pollution created by the dam itself? Does the increased amount of electrical power balance the loss of historical, artistic, and natural treasures? Does it balance the loss of a million homes? The Chinese have worked to clean up pollution near the dam. They have created breeding farms for endangered fish. Will this be enough? It may take many decades to tell.

"We absolutely cannot relax our guard against ecological and environmental security problems sparked by the Three Gorges project. We cannot win passing economic prosperity at the cost of the environment."

—*Wang Xiaofeng, dam official, 2007*

7 Nanomachines

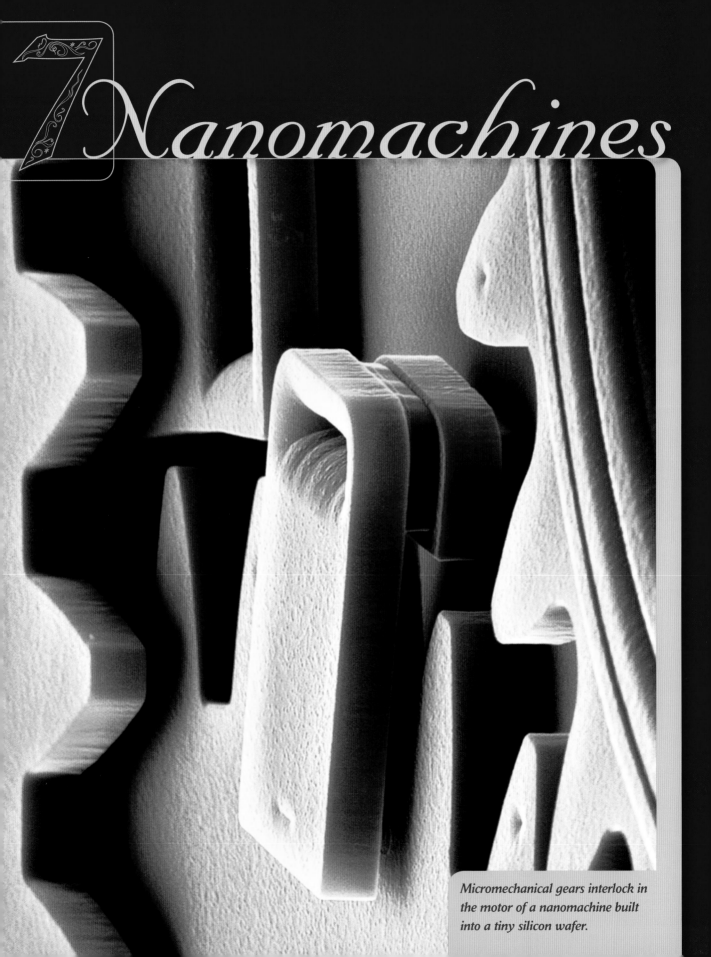

Micromechanical gears interlock in the motor of a nanomachine built into a tiny silicon wafer.

GIANT BUILDINGS, VAST BRIDGES, AND HUGE TUNNELS—GREAT SIZE SEEMS TO BE A PART OF THE WONDER OF ENGINEERING. BUT WHAT ABOUT VERY TINY MACHINES? WHAT ABOUT MACHINES THAT ARE SO SMALL THEY CAN BE SEEN ONLY THROUGH A MICROSCOPE? THIS IS THE WORLD OF NANOENGINEERING.

The word *nano* comes from the Greek word for "dwarf." A nanometer is 1 billionth of a meter, or about 400 millionths of an inch. This is very, very small. A single human hair is about 100,000 nanometers thick.

A nanoengineer builds machines that are extremely tiny. Some nanoengineers have created machines that are only 100 nanometers wide. A thousand of them could fit across the width of a single hair. Nanoengineers have to work with individual atoms, just as other engineers work with bricks and steel girders.

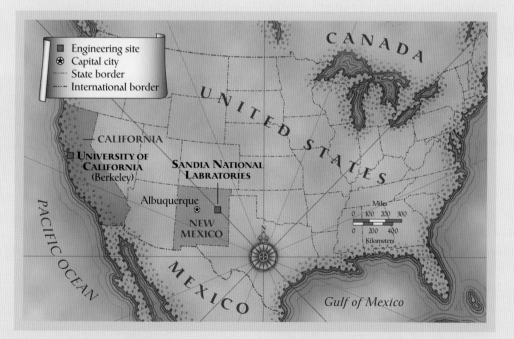

Engineers of the Imagination

U.S. physicist Richard Feynman first suggested the idea for nanomachines in 1959. He had given a lecture on the possibility of building devices atom by atom. Eric Drexler, another physicist, developed the idea. Beginning in 1977, Drexler wrote a series of books about nanoengineering. It was a great idea, but no one knew how to move individual atoms and put them in place.

The invention of the scanning tunneling microscope (STM) helped solve this problem. This machine allowed scientists to look at individual atoms and move them. In 1990 researchers at International Business Machines (IBM) used this machine to spell out the computer company logo one letter at a time. It took thirty-five atoms of the gas xenon. It was the first time anyone had created a structure by moving individual atoms.

Atoms of xenon gas spell out the IBM logo on a nickel plate.

Above left: *Sandia National Laboratories created an early micromachine with six gears. A tiny spider mite seems huge next to this micromachine.* **Below left:** *Each gear is smaller in diameter than a human hair.*

FROM IMAGINATION TO REALITY

Engineers have not yet created practical nanomachines. They have developed micromachines. They have microscopic gears, wheels, and axles. These machines are no larger than a speck of dust. Engineers at the U.S. Department of Energy's Sandia National Laboratories in Albuquerque, New Mexico, have created a micromachine that has gears. Each one is smaller in diameter than a human hair.

Making a tiny engine powerful enough to run one of these machines is a much more complicated problem. In 1988 engineers at the University

> *"Nanotechnology will let us build computers that are incredibly powerful. We'll have more power in the volume of a sugar cube than exists in the entire world today."*
> —Ralph Merkle, U.S. scientist, 2000

of California–Berkeley created the world's first micromotor. It was just 100 microns (100,000 nanometers) across. The motor was powered by static electricity. This is the same force that sometimes makes a little spark when you touch something after walking across a carpet. This energy made tiny gears spin at high speeds, but it wasn't powerful enough to do any useful work.

Right: *This micromachine is one hundred times thinner than a piece of paper.* Below left: *A micromotor drives a small gear, which turns a gear about ten times larger in diameter.* Below right: *Parts of a microengine appear with a grain of pollen (center) and clumps of red blood cells (left and right) to demonstrate their size.*

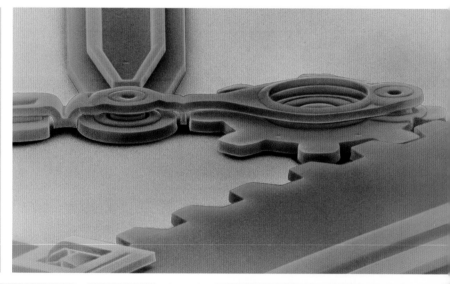

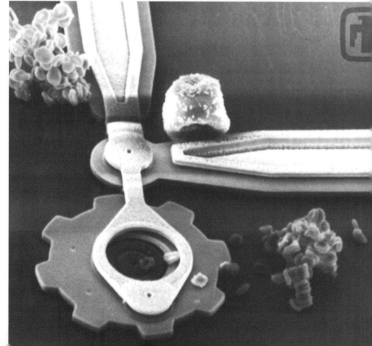

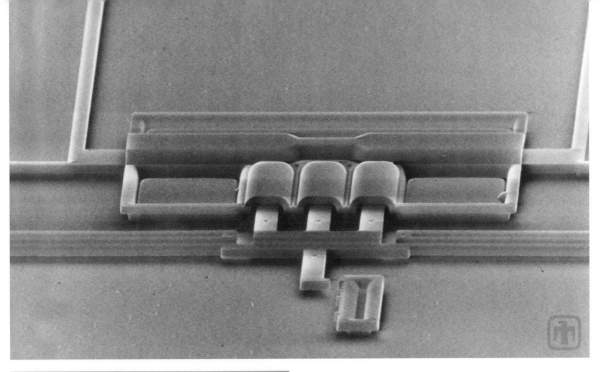

Top: *Jeffry J. Sniegowski developed this microsteam engine. An electric current heats water inside the three tiny cylinders, and the resulting steam pushes the pistons out.* Bottom: *Dr. Alex Zettl stands in front of an illustration of his nanomotor. Its gold rotor paddles spin on a carbon tube.*

More recently, Sandia has been developing much more powerful micromachines. They include a tiny steam engine invented by Jeffry J. Sniegowski. It is only 6 microns long and 2 microns wide. It features a tiny piston run by a bubble of water vapor. This steam engine produces much more power than earlier tiny engines. It can actually run a micromachine. Manufacturers may be able to produce these engines very cheaply, perhaps for only ten or fifteen dollars each.

In 2003 Dr. Alex Zettl, a physicist at the University of California–Berkeley created the first nanomotor. It is a tiny electric motor so small it can fit on the back of a cold virus. About two hundred of them could fit on a human hair. So far, all the motor can do is spin a tiny rotor. It has not produced enough power to run a machine. Engineers are certain, however, that they will soon develop much more powerful electric nanomotors.

Researchers hope that a tiny chip like this one might one day allow people blinded by certain eye diseases to see again. The chip carries a micromachine that mimics the way that the eye delivers information to the brain.

MICROSCIENCE AND MEDICINE

Tiny nanomachines might be able to clean rivers and the air by gathering pollutants, the way bees collect pollen. They might even be able to re-create themselves. Each nanomachine could make hundreds of thousands of exact copies of itself.

Doctors especially are very excited about micromachines and nanomachines. These machines would be far smaller than a blood cell. They could be injected into the human body. Cruising through the body, these machines could perform all sorts of tasks to keep a person healthy.

Sniegowski's micro steam engine could be connected to tiny tweezers or scalpels. It could operate on individual cells within a human body. It would be like a tiny robot doctor. "Eye surgery, neurosurgery [operating on nerve cells], certain areas of brain surgery come to mind," says Paul McWhorter, an engineer who helped develop the

NATURAL *Nanomachines*

Medical nanomachines are inspired by the body's own natural nanomachines. An example would be the white blood cells. They constantly roam throughout the body to destroy invading bacteria and foreign particles. This is the kind of job that nanomachines could do. Unlike the white blood cells, however, nanomachines could be programmed to perform very specific tasks. For example, they could search for certain types of damaged or diseased tissue. Or they could be programmed to deliver medicine to only one type of cell.

Left: *A micromachine uses a tiny pair of mechanical jaws to catch a single human blood cell. A machine like this might be used to repair cells or to deliver drugs to specific kinds of cells.* Right: *This illustration shows a proposed nanomachine repairing a strand of DNA.*

steam engine. "Right now we're looking for neurosurgeons and eye surgeons to tell us what they really need." Perhaps, someday doctors could inject thousands or even millions of these tiny machines into the bloodstream. There they will cruise like miniature submarines, looking for damaged or unhealthy cells and repairing them. They could cure people before they even knew they were sick.

Other nanomachines might be able to build molecules of any medicine, atom by atom. The machines may even be able to build other tiny machines exactly like themselves, reproducing like the cells in the human body.

In early 2009, scientists from the United States and China created a two-armed nanomachine. The machine is only 150 by 50 by 8 nanometers. It will be able to build molecules of deoxyribonucleic acid (DNA) one atom at a time. The DNA molecule is the genetic building block of living things. The nanomachine might serve as a factory for assembling new types of materials and medicines.

"There is no doubt that nanotechnology has the potential to make the world a better place."
—*Andrew Maynard, the Project on Emerging Nanotechnologies, 2007*

Timeline

ca. 2560 B.C. Egyptians build the Great Pyramid of Giza. Originally 481 feet (147 m) high, it was the tallest building in the world for more than thirty-eight hundred years.

1854 Elisha Otis invents the steel elevator cable, making it practical to build tall buildings.

1869 The French construct the Suez Canal.

1880 The French begin building a canal through Panama, but the work has to be abandoned.

Great Britain and France begin digging an English Channel Tunnel.

1884 The Washington Monument is completed in Washington, D.C. It is 555 feet (169 m) tall.

1885 Engineers erect the first true skyscraper (a tall building with a steel supporting skeleton). It is 138 feet (42 m) tall.

1889 Gustave Eiffel erects the Eiffel Tower for the Paris Exposition. It is 1,024 feet (312 m) tall.

1901 The tallest brick building ever built is Philadelphia's City Hall.

1903 The United States begins work on the Panama Canal.

1914 The first ship passes through the Panama Canal.

1930 Workers complete the Chrysler Building.

1931 The Empire State Building, at 1,453 feet (443 m), becomes the world's tallest building. It holds the title for forty-one years.

1937 The Golden Gate Bridge opens to the public. It is the longest suspension bridge in the world at the time.

1959 U.S. physicist Richard Feynman suggests the concept of nanomachines.

1961 President John F. Kennedy commits the United States to landing on the Moon within ten years.

1964   The Verrazano-Narrows Bridge in New York exceeds the Golden Gate Bridge in length.

1967   NASA launches its first test flight of the Saturn V rocket.

1969   *Apollo 11* astronauts—launched from Earth by the Saturn V rocket—land on the Moon.

1974   Britain and France again attempt to dig an English Channel Tunnel. It is abandoned due to politics and lack of money.

1977   Physicist Eric Drexler writes the first of a series of books about nanotechnology.

1986   The World Trade Center towers in New York, at 1,368 feet (417 m), become the world's tallest buildings.

1988   Engineers build the first operating micromotor. It is about the width of a human hair.

1990   IBM engineers create the company logo from thiry-five xenon atoms.

1994   The English Channel Tunnel—officially the Eurotunnel—opens.

1999   The United States transfers ownership of the Panama Canal to Panama.

2003   Alex Zettl makes the first operating nanomotor.

2006   China finishes construction on the Three Gorges Dam on the Yangtze River.

2009   Scientists from the United States and China create a two-armed nanomachine.

CHOOSE AN EIGHTH WONDER

Now that you've read about the seven engineering wonders of the modern world, do a little research to choose an eighth wonder. You may enjoy working with a friend.

To do your research, look at some of the websites and books listed on pages 76 and 77. Use the Internet and library books to look for more information on some of the other engineers and structures mentioned in the book. What are some other cities around the world that might have amazing feats of engineering? Look for things that
- ***are built to survive extreme conditions***
- ***used new building techniques or designs***
- ***are exceptionally large or small***

You might even try gathering photos and writing your own chapter on the eighth wonder!

GLOSSARY

architect: a person who designs buildings

canal: an artificial river or channel connecting two bodies of water

cofferdam: a four-sided dam meant to keep the surrounding water of a river, lake, or ocean from a work area

engineer: a person who puts science and technology to practical use

gigawatt: a measure of electrical power equal to a billion watts (a typical lightbulb is 75 watts)

horsepower: a measure of mechanical energy equal to 746 watts

hydroelectricity: electricity generated by falling water

isthmus: a narrow neck of land connecting two larger bodies of land

lock: a section of a canal, closed off with gates, in which boats can be raised or lowered by raising or lowering the water level within it

micromachine: a machine the size of which is measured in micrometers

micrometer: one-millionth of a meter; also called a micron. The period at the end of this sentence is about 397 microns wide.

nanoengineering: making machines and other devices that are measured in nanometers

nanomachine: a tiny machine that is measured in nanometers

nanometer: one-billionth of a meter. A sheet of paper is about 100,000 nanometers thick.

skyscraper: a very tall building, usually more than twenty stories

suspension bridge: a bridge with a roadway suspended from cables that are supported by towers and anchored at either end

thrust: a measure of the force that propels a rocket or jet

Source Notes

9   Jonathan Goldman, *The Empire State Building Book* (New York: St. Martin's Press, 1980), 30.

13   Ibid, 132.

13   Helen Keller, quoted in "63 Candles, 102 Floors, and One Million Stories," *Interview*, May 1994, 1, available online at http://findarticles.com/p/articles/mi_m1285/is_n5 _v24/ai_15409303 (July 27, 2009).

14   Herbert Hoover, "Message on the Completion of the Empire State Building," The American Presidency Project, May 1, 1931, available online at http://www.presidency .ucsb.edu/ws/index.php?pid=22636 (July 27, 2009).

22   Leigh Mercer, "A Few More Palindromes," *Notes & Queries* 193 (November 1948); 193.

24   Theodore Roosevelt, *Theodore Roosevelt: An Autobiography* (New York: Macmillan, 1913), 543.

33   Joseph Strauss, quoted in Robert G. Torricelli, Andrew Carroll, and Doris Kearns, *In Our Own Words* (New York: Simon and Schuster, 2000), 104–105.

39   William Gladstone, "The Channel Tunnel," speech given to the House of Commons, June 27, 1888, available online at http://en.wikisource.org/wiki/The_Channel_Tunnel (July 27, 2009).

43   Francois Mitterrand of France, quoted in "Channel Tunnel Handshake Links Britain, France," *Chicago Sun-Times,* December 2, 1990, available online at http://www .highbeam.com/doc/1P2-4029385.html (July 27, 2009).

45   NASA, "The Decision to Go to the Moon: President John F. Kennedy's May 25, 1961 Speech before a Joint Session of Congress," *NASA History*, March 24, 2004, http:// history.nasa.gov/moondec.html (November 2008).

47   Guenter Wendt, 1968, quoted at http://www.spacequotations.com/rocketryquotes .html (July 27, 2009).

45   NASA, "John F. Kennedy Moon Speech—Rice Stadium, September 12, 1962, *NASA JSC*, November 30, 2004, http://er.jsc.nasa.gov/seh/ricetalk.htm (November 2008).

50   Neil A. Armstrong, "One Small Step," *NASA*, July 20, 1969, available online at http:// history.nasa.gov/alsj/a11/a11.step.html (July 27, 2009).

59   "Exhibition," *China Three Gorges Project,* 2003, available online at http://www.ctgpc .com/exibition/exibition_a.php (July 27, 2009).

61   Wang Xiaofeng, quoted in Jane Macartney, "Three Gorges Dam is a Disaster in the Making, China Admits" *Times Online,* September 27, 2007, available online at http:// www.timesonline.co.uk/tol/news/world/article2537279.ece (July 27, 2009).

66   Ralph Merkle, "Nanotechnology: Designs for the Future," Ubiquity, n.d., available online at http://www.acm.org/ubiquity/interviews/r_merkle_1.html (July 27, 2009).

69 Richard Lipken, "Micro Steam Engine Makes Forceful Debut," *Science News*, September 25, 1993, available online at BNET, http://findarticles.com/p/articles/mi_m1200/is_n13_v144/ai_14492587 (July 27, 2009).

69 Andrew Maynard, "Quote of the Day," *Blog~Nano*, November 6, 2007, available online at http://nanoscale-materials-and-nanotechnolog.blogspot.com/2007/11/quote-of-day.html (July 27, 2009).

SELECTED BIBLIOGRAPHY

Berga, Luis, J. M. Buil, E. Bofill, J. C. De Ceu, J. A. Garcia Perez, G. Mañueco, J. Polimon, A. Soriano, and J. Yague, eds. *Dams and Reservoirs, Societies and Environment in the 21st Century*. London: Taylor and Francis, 2006.

Chester, Michael. *Joseph Strauss, Builder of the Golden Gate Bridge*. New York: Putnam, 1965.

Drexler, Eric. *Engines of Creation*. New York: Anchor, 1987.

Featherston, Drew. *The Chunnel: The Amazing Story of the Undersea Crossing of the English Channel*. New York: Crown, 1997.

Kingwell, Mark. *Nearest Thing to Heaven: The Empire State Building and American Dreams*. New Haven, CT: Yale University Press, 2006.

McCullough, David. *The Path between the Seas: The Creation of the Panama Canal 1870–1914*. Tappan, NJ: Touchstone, 1978.

Reynolds, David West. *Apollo: The Epic Journey to the Moon*. New York: Harcourt, 2002.

FURTHER READING AND WEBSITES

Books

Behnke, Alison. *China in Pictures*. Minneapolis: Twenty-First Century Books, 2003. Learn more about China, home of the Three Gorges Dam.

Chaikin, Andrew. *A Man on the Moon: The Voyages of the Apollo Astronauts*. New York: Penguin, 1995. This is the complete story of the epic Apollo missions to the Moon.

Donovan, Sandy. *The Channel Tunnel*. Minneapolis: Twenty-First Century Books, 2003. This is a history of the tunnel and of the engineering feats that made it possible.

DuTemple, Leslie. *The Panama Canal*. Minneapolis: Twenty-First Century Books, 2003. This book tells the exciting story of how the canal was planned, excavated, and built.

Johnson, Rebecca L. *Nanotechnology*. Minneapolis: Lerner Publications Company, 2006. Learn about ultra-small materials and machines with varied and remarkable properties.

MacDonald, Donald. *Golden Gate Bridge: History and Design of an Icon*. San Francisco: Chronicle Books, 2008. This book is an easy-to-understand account of how the bridge was designed and constructed.

Mattern, Joanne. *The Chunnel*. Farmington Hills, MI: Blackbirch Press, 2003. This book describes in detail how the first railroad tunnel underneath the English Channel was built.

McCauley, David. *Unbuilding*. New York: Houghton Mifflin, 1987. A step-by-step explanation with many pages of wonderful drawings shows how the Empire State Building was constructed.

McPherson, Stephanie Sammartino. *Theodore Roosevelt*. Minneapolis: Twenty-First Century Books, 2005. This biography of Theodore Roosevelt describes some of the complicated international policy behind the building of the Panama Canal.

Miller, Ron. *Rockets*. Minneapolis: Twenty-First Century Books, 2008. This book tells the story of rockets, from their beginnings as toys to their use as weapons, and details their starring role in space travel.

Parker, Matthew. *Panama Fever: The Epic Story of One of the Greatest Human Achievements of All Time—the Building of the Panama Canal*. New York: Doubleday, 2008. An exciting history of the building of the Panama Canal describes in detail how it came to be and its great cost in resources and human lives.

Scientific American. *Understanding Nanotechnology*. New York: Grand Central Publishing, 2002. This book explains how nanomachines work and how they will be used in medicine, space exploration, and many other areas.

Woods, Michael, and Mary B. Woods. *Ancient Construction: From Tents to Towers*. Minneapolis: Twenty-First Century Books, 2000. Follow the history of construction from basic shelters to amazing feats of engineering like the Golden Gate Bridge.

Websites

Empire State Building

http://www.esbnyc.com/index2.cfm?noflash=1
The official site of the Empire Building contains history, unusual facts, and photos.

The English Channel Tunnel

http://www.eurotunnel.com
This is the official website for Eurotunnel with much information about its history and daily operation.

The Golden Gate Bridge

http://www.goldengatebridge.org/
The official site for the Golden Gate Bridge gives information on its history and daily operation.

Micromachines

http://mems.sandia.gov/
This site, run by Sandia National Laboratories, describes its work in developing micromachines and nanomachines and has lots of amazing photos.

The Panama Canal

http://www.pancanal.com/eng/index.html
This site is run by the Panama Canal Authority. It describes the canal, its history, and future.

The Saturn V Moon Rocket

http://www.apollosaturn.com/saturnv.htm
This site contains detailed information about the Saturn V, its history, and uses. It also contains a great many photos and drawings.

Seven Wonders of the Modern World

http://www.asce.org/history/seven_wonders.cfm
These seven greatest achievements of modern engineering were chosen by the American Society of Civil Engineers.

The Three Gorges Dam

http://www.ctgpc.com/
This is the official Chinese website for the Three Gorges Dam project.

INDEX

Akashi Kaikyo Bridge, 33
Aldrin, Edwin "Buzz," 51
Apollo spacecraft, 47, 48
architects: Lamb, William, 9–10; Morrow, Irving, 29
Ares V rocket, 53
Armstrong, Neil, 51

balloon travel, 38
bar codes, 49
Beijing, China, 56
Beijing National Grand Theater, 56
Bering Strait, 35
"bird's nest" stadium, 56
Blanchard, Jean Pierre, 38
Blériot, Louis, 38
brick and stone construction, 8
bridges, suspension, 28
Bush, George W., 53

California Gold Rush, 17
canals, 21, *See also* Panama Canal
Cape Canaveral Air Force Station, 45
Carter, Jimmy, 25
Channel Tunnel (Chunnel), 36; construction, 39–42; cost, 39; facts, 42; location, 37; modern status, 43; origins, 37–39; website, 77
China, 56
Chrysler, Walter, 8–9, 11–14
Chrysler Building, 9, 11–14
churches, 7
cofferdams, 30
Collins, Michael, 51
Colombia, 20
Crystal Palace Exposition, 9

dams, 60, *See also* Three Gorges Dam
De Gamond, Thome, 38, 39
de Lesseps, Ferdinand, 19
deoxyribonucleic acid (DNA), 69
Drexler, Eric, 64

Eiffel Tower, 7, 8
elevators, 9
Empire State Building, 6; construction, 10–14; cost, 13; facts, 13; location, 7; modern status, 15; origins, 9–10; Run Up, 15; website, 77
engineering, 4–5
engineers: De Gamond, Thome, 38, 39; de Lesseps, Ferdinand, 19; Goethals, George Washington, 20–22; McWhorter, Paul, 68–69; Stevens, John Frank, 20; Strauss, Joseph, 28–29; Wallace, John Findley, 20
English Channel, 35, 37–43
Eurotunnel. *See* Channel Tunnel (Chunnel)

Feynman, Richard, 64
Flatiron Building, 8
Flying Cloud (ship), 18
Forbidden City (Beijing), 56

Gatun Dam, 23, 24
Goddard, Robert H., 46
Goethals, George Washington, 20–22
Golden Gate Bridge, 26; construction, 29–32; deaths, 29; facts, 32; location, 27; opening, 32–33; origins, 27–29; website, 77
Grand Canal of China, 56
Great Pyramid at Giza, 7
Great Wall of China, 56
gunpowder, 46

Hine, Lewis W., 12
Hoover Dam, 59
hydroelectric power, 55

insecticides, 22

Kennedy, John F., 45
Kennedy Space Center, 45
King Kong (movie), 15

Lamb, William, 9–10
locks, 21

McWhorter, Paul, 68–69
medicine and nanoengineering, 68–69
micromachines, 64–66
micromotors, 65–67
moon landing, 51
Morrow, Irving, 29
Moscoso, Mireya, 25

nanoengineering, 63; and medicine, 68–69; micromachines, 64–66; micromotors, 65–67; natural nanomachines, 68; scanning tunneling microscope, 64; website, 77
New York City, 6–15

Otis, Elisha Graves, 9

Panama, 17–25
Panama Canal, 16; construction, 22–24; cost, 25; Culebra Cut, 23; deaths, 22; facts, 25; location, 17; modern status, 25; origins, 18–19; website, 77
Petronas Towers, 15

Raskob, John, 8–9, 10, 14
rockets, 46, *See also* Saturn V rocket
Roosevelt, Franklin D., 33
Roosevelt, Theodore, 20–21

safety, 29
Saint Mary's Church, 7
Samphire Hoe, 41
Sandia National Laboratories, 65, 67
San Francisco, 27–35
Saturn V rocket, 44, 52; assembly, 49; challenges, 46–47; displays, 53; facts, 53; F-1 engines, 5, 47;

launch, 50; location, 45; moon landing, 51; stages, 48; website, 77

scanning tunneling microscope, 64

Sears Tower, 14–15

Seikan Tunnel, 40

seven wonders of the modern world, 77

skyscrapers, 8, *See also* Empire State Building

Sleepless in Seattle (movie), 15

Smith, Alfred, 10

Sniegowski, Jeffry J., 67, 68

steel frame construction, 8

Stevens, John Frank, 20

Strauss, Joseph, 28–29

Suez Canal, 19

superbridges, 35

suspension bridges, 28

Taipei 101, 15

Three Gorges Dam, 54, 55–56; construction, 57–59; controversy, 59–61; location, 55; website, 77

Torrijos, Omar, 25

tunneling, 38–39, 40–41

units of measure, 64

University of California–Berkeley, 65–66

Vehicle Assembly Building, 49

Verrazano-Narrows Bridge, 33

von Braun, Wernher, 47

V-2 rockets, 47

Wallace, John Findley, 20

Washington Monument, 7

Weber, Hamilton, 13

Willis Tower, 15

World Trade Center towers, 14

Yangtze River, 54–61

yellow fever, 22

Zettl, Alex, 67

ABOUT THE AUTHOR

Hugo Award-winning author and illustrator Ron Miller specializes in books about science. He has written *The Elements: What You Really Want To Know* and *Special Effects: An Introduction to Movie Magic*. His original paintings can be found in collections all over the world. Miller lives in Virginia.

PHOTO ACKNOWLEDGMENTS

The images in this book are used with the permission of: NASA/MSFC, pp. 5, 44, 46, 47, 48 (all); © Cameron Davidson/Photographer's Choice RR/Getty Images, p. 6; © Laura Westlund/Independent Picture Service, pp. 7, 17, 27, 37, 41 (bottom), 45, 55, 63; Library of Congress, pp. 8 (LC–USZ62–127120), 23 (right, LC–USZ62–117222); © Archive Photos/Hulton Archive/Getty Images, p. 9; Milstein Division of United States History, Local History and Genealogy, The New York Public Library, Astor, Lenox and Tilden Foundations, p. 10 (top); AP Photo, pp. 10 (bottom), 31 (top and bottom left), 33, 58 (bottom left); Photography Collection, Miriam and Ira D. Wallach Division of Art, Prints and Photographs, The New York Public Library, Astor, Lenox and Tilden Foundations, p. 11; National Archives, p. 12 (top, 69-RH-4K-1), 22 (185-G-640-A-13); © Lewis W. Hine/George Eastman House/Getty Images, p. 12 (bottom); © Marta Johnson, p. 13; © Steffen Thalemann/Iconica/Getty Images, p. 14; © Spencer Platt/Getty Images, p. 15 (left); © Grant Faint/The Image Bank/Getty Images, p. 15 (right); © age fotostock/SuperStock, pp. 16, 35; © North Wind Picture Archives, p. 18; © London Stereoscopic Company/Hulton Archive/Getty Images, p. 19 (top); © Brown Brothers, pp. 19 (bottom), 20, 23 (left); © Hulton Archive/Getty Images, p. 21 (bottom); © Nevada Wier/The Image Bank/Getty Images, pp. 21 (top), 72 (bottom center); AP Photo/Tomas van Houtryve, p. 24 (top); © Time & Life Pictures/Getty Images, p. 24 (bottom); © Rodrigo Arangua/AFP/Getty Images, p. 25; © Brian Lawrence/Photographer's Choice/Getty Images, p. 26; San Francisco History Center, San Francisco Public Library, pp. 28, 29 (top), 30, 32; Courtesy of The Bancroft Library, University of California, Berkeley, Construction Photographs of the Golden Gate Bridge, #1905.14256 no. 1-102, p. 29 (bottom); © Stephen Finn/Alamy, p. 31 (bottom right); AP Photo/Doug Atkins, p. 34; © qaphotos.com/Alamy, pp. 36, 42 (top); © Popperfoto/Getty Images, p. 38; © Joseph McKeown/Hulton Archive/Getty Images, p. 39 (left); © General Photographic Agency/Hulton Archive/Getty Images, p. 39 (right); © Graham Wood/Evening Standard/Hulton Archive/Getty Images, p. 40; © Manor Photography/Alamy, p. 41 (top); © Jim Byrne/QAPHOTOS, p. 42 (bottom); © Philippe Huguen/AFP/Getty Images, p. 43; NASA/KSC, pp. 49, 51 (top); © Ralph Morse/Time & Life Pictures/Getty Images, p. 50; NASA/JSC, pp. 51 (bottom), 52, 72 (bottom right); © Altrendo Travel/Getty Images, p. 53; Imaginechina via AP Images, pp. 54, 72 (bottom Left); © Travel Ink/Gallo Images/Getty Images, p. 56; © Keren Su/China Span/Alamy, p. 57; AP Photo/Greg Baker, pp. 58 (top), 61 (top); © Goh Chai Hin/AFP/Getty Images, p. 58 (bottom right); AP Photo/John Leicester, p. 59; © Guang Niu/Getty Images, p. 60; © China Photos/Getty Images, p. 61 (bottom); © Sandia National Laboratories/Photo Researchers, Inc., pp. 62, 66 (top), 69 (left), 72 (center right); © Science VU/IBMRL/Visuals Unlimited, Inc., p. 64; Sandia National Laboratories, pp. 65 (top), 66 (bottom left and bottom right), 67 (top); © George Musil/Visuals Unlimited, Inc., p. 65 (bottom); Roy Kaltschmidt/Lawrence Berkeley National Laboratory , p. 67 (bottom); © Randy Montoya/Sandia National Laboratories/Getty Images, p. 68; © Victor Habbick Visions/Photo Researchers, Inc., p. 69 (right); © iStockphoto.com/Dean Birinyi, p. 72 (top left); © Denis Charlet/AFP/Getty Images, p. 72 (top center); © Ron Chapple Studios/Dreamstime.com, p. 72 (top right).

Front Cover: NASA/JSC (top left); © Sandia National Laboratories/Photo Researchers, Inc. (top center); © Ron Chapple Studios/Dreamstime.com (top right); © Denis Charlet/AFP/Getty Images (center); © iStockphoto.com/Dean Birinyi (bottom left); © Nevada Wier/The Image Bank/Getty Images (bottom center); Imaginechina via AP Images (bottom right).